Grandma Elephant's in charge

For Agnes from me,
and for Holly from the elephants
M.J.

For all of George's grandmas, Hazel,
Kathy, Pauline and Gillian
I.B.

First published 2003 by Walker Books Ltd
87 Vauxhall Walk, London SE11 5HJ

This edition published 2010

2 4 6 8 10 9 7 5 3 1

Text © 2003 Martin Jenkins
Illustrations © 2003 Ivan Bates
The moral rights of the author and illustrator
have been asserted

This book has been typeset in Bembo Educational

Printed in China

British Library Cataloguing in Publication Data:
a catalogue record for this book is available from the British Library

ISBN 978-1-4063-1859-3

www.walker.co.uk

Grandma Elephant's in charge

Martin Jenkins

illustrated by Ivan Bates

WALKER BOOKS
AND SUBSIDIARIES

LONDON · BOSTON · SYDNEY · AUCKLAND

Most elephants live in families.

And most elephant families are big
(just like elephants).

There'll probably be two or three babies,
forever playing push-me-pull-you,

or peekaboo, or anything else
that makes a lot of noise.

And each of the babies might have
an older brother or sister – handy
for playing king of the castle on!

And then there are the mums.
They look after their own babies,
and each other's too – keeping
an eye on them to make sure
they don't wander off, and
scolding them when they get
too boisterous.

But that's not all. The most
important member of an
elephant family is …

Grandma!

Grandma's been around
a long time and
she knows lots of
important things.

She knows where
the water holes are
when it hasn't rained
and the easiest places
to cross the big river
when it has rained.

She knows
where to find
the juiciest melons ...

and knows the best path
up the cliff to the salt lick.

It's not surprising that she's
the one in charge.

She doesn't make a big
song-and-dance about it,
though. Just a flick
of the ear or a snort
or two, and a
rumble,
rumble,
rumble,
deep down in
her throat,
seem to be
enough to tell
all the other
elephants
what
to do.

If she stops, they all stop. If she moves,
they all move. And if there's any sign
of danger, you can be sure she'll be
the first to investigate and the first

to decide what the family should do.
They might all run away … or they
might take a stand.
Or Grandma might

c–h–a–r–g–e.

If she charges with her head up
and ears flapping, waving her
trunk and making a great to-do,
then she's probably bluffing.
But if her head's down,
her trunk's tucked under and
she's not making any noise,
then she means business.
In that case, whatever it is
that has annoyed her had
better watch out.

And once all the commotion's over, everyone can settle back down to feeding and snoozing and messing about – safe in the knowledge that Grandma has sorted things out again.

So if you're an elephant, there's one thing you should never forget. Wherever you are and whatever you're doing …

Grandma's in charge!

More about elephants

Elephants are the biggest land animals of all. A big male can weigh six tonnes – as much as 100 people.

Elephants can live for up to sixty-five years, but don't usually have any more babies once they're older than fifty or so.

Elephants move around a lot. It's important for them to have good memories so that the family doesn't get lost when they return to places they haven't visited for a very long time.

A charging elephant can run at 40 kph – that's faster than the fastest human.

Elephants are very fond of things like melons but feed mainly on grass, leaves and twigs. Adults eat about 1.5 tonnes of food each day.
Salt licks are places where the earth is full of minerals. Lots of animals eat the minerals, which help to keep them healthy.

Adult male elephants don't normally stay with the family. Instead they move about by themselves or with other males.

There are two kinds of living elephant. The elephants in this book are African elephants; the other kind are Asian elephants, which live in South and South-east Asia. Elephants were once found almost everywhere in Africa, but now they have disappeared from many of the places where they used to live. This is because they have been hunted and people have taken their land for farming.

Twenty years ago there were
over 1,000,000 African elephants.
Now there may be only
half that number.

Elephant mothers have only one baby at a time. They give birth every three or four years. Elephants don't become

fully grown until they're ten years old or more. The mothers in the herd are usually sisters.

Index

About the Author

Martin Jenkins is a conservation biologist and author of the award-winning *The Emperor's Egg*, amongst other children's books. Martin has seen wild elephants many times, but the first time he saw them was in Kenya. "There was a big family of them making their way across the savanna," says Martin. "I'll never forget them, strolling across the plains without a care in the world – it was magic."

About the Illustrator

Ivan Bates has illustrated a number
of children's books, including
Do Like a Duck Does.
About this book, Ivan says, "I have
always found elephants fascinating
creatures capable of both extreme
strength and tenderness. This combined
with their almighty stature and set in
those wonderful, vast land and
skyscapes, makes them
a joy to draw."

There are 10 titles in the
READ AND DISCOVER series.
Which ones have you read?

Available from all good booksellers

www.walker.co.uk

FOR THE BEST CHILDREN'S BOOKS, LOOK FOR THE BEAR.